AF674441

Phonics Activity

Book 2

Om KIDZ
An imprint of Om Books International

WORD BUILDER

Look at the pictures and say their names out loud. Then, fill in the blanks with the correct letter. What is the common sound you hear?

b ___ t

h ___ t

c ___ t

m ___ n

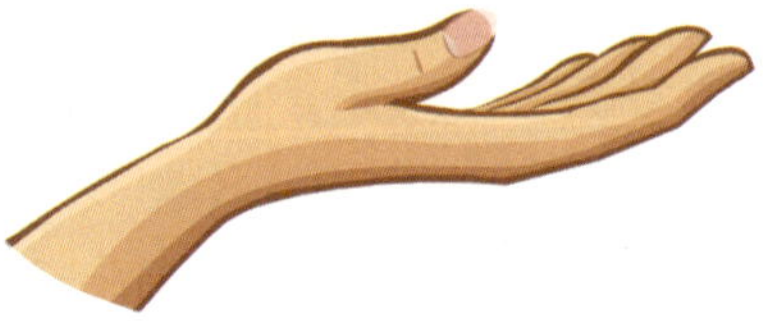

h ___ ___ d

f ___ n

Now, read these words aloud.

that rat black bad land ant apple had an sand happy can

MUMBLE JUMBLE

Look at these pictures. What do you call them? Unscramble the letters and write the correct words below. Then, read the words aloud.

t d e a

___ ___ ___ ___

s k e n a

___ ___ ___ ___ ___

k e r a

___ ___ ___ ___

g t a e

___ ___ ___ ___

k e l a

___ ___ ___ ___

c e a k

___ ___ ___ ___

Now, read these words aloud.

ate　day　make　take　shake　came　date　brake

SSHH!

Help Ollie the Octopus complete the words on the bubbles using 'sh' or 'ch'.

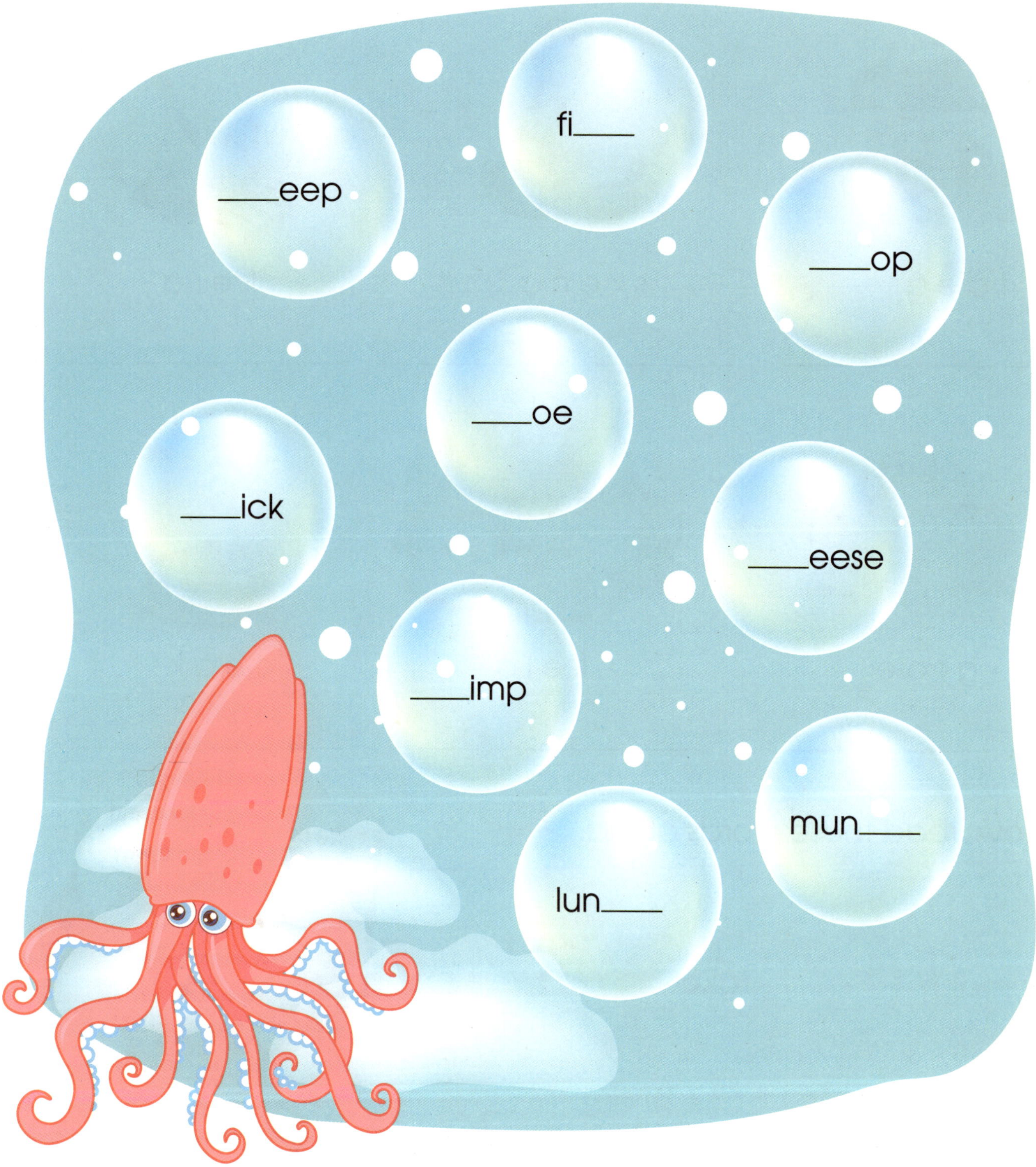

PHONIC FISHING

Fish out the letters from the lake and drop them on the blanks to complete the words. You can use a letter more than once.

CRABBY'S CROSSWORD

Help Crust the Crab fill in the crossword by naming the clues.

THE INCOMPLETE MATCH

Help Sparkles the Starfish unscramble the 'th' words below.

thhgruo ____________

tehvri ____________

erhte ____________

rwoht ____________

rshuth ____________

rohent ____________

WORD SORTER

Help Goldie the Goldfish match the word shells to the correct bowl.

EEPS!

Complete the words below using 'ee' or 'ea'.

b ______ ch	gr ______ n
l ______ f	______ l
m ______ l	b ______ k
ch ______ se	gr ______ se
fr ______ ze	br ______ ze

SEAWEED SELECTION

Choose the correct letters from the seaweeds to fill in the blanks below.

The mermaid is watching a gh______ movie.

The y______ of an egg is yellow in colour.

Dolphins are found alm______ everywhere.

F______ dances are fun to watch.

Please p______ this letter, will you?

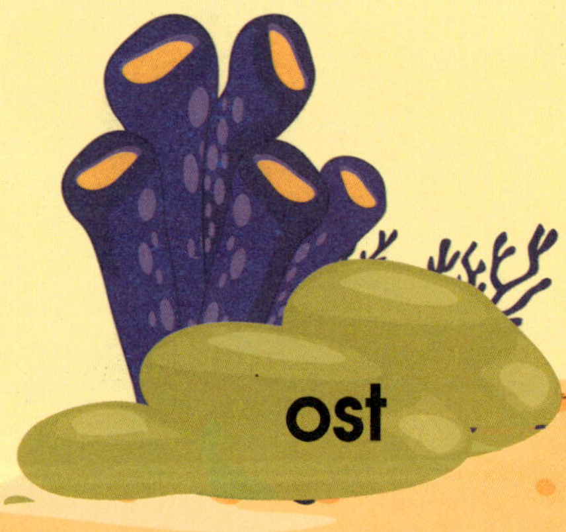

OCTOWORDS

Otto the Octopus is juggling with 'oa' words, but he can't catch the right ones! Can you circle all the words with 'oa' in them?

SILENT MATCH

Unscramble the letters on the submarine to form new words. Then, circle the silent letter in them.

WORD HUNT

Help Sally the Seahorse hunt for words in the grid below.
Look for words that have the same letters as the shells.

c	b	t	r	a	i	n	g
l	b	b	c	d	e	f	d
a	l	n	o	w	a	y	e
y	p	m	d	a	y	h	f
q	p	r	s	i	j	i	g
m	a	y	t	t	a	i	l
y	y	z	u	v	w	x	k
a	b	p	l	a	y	c	t
d	e	l	k	l	m	n	r
f	s	a	i	l	p	o	a
p	a	i	l	q	r	s	y
g	h	n	i	s	a	y	j

PERFECT FIT

Help Frodo the Frog choose the correct word to fill in the blanks.

The rabbit's ________ is furry. (hare/hair)

Here are a ________ of turtles. (pare/pair)

Help the octopus up these ________. (stairs/stares)

The little jellyfish seems hurt and in ________. (pane/pain)

They call her a ________ fish. (plane/plain)

The lion's ________ is beautiful. (mane/main)

SILENT ADDITION

Help Wally the Whale add 'e' and change the words on the bubbles. Say the new words out loud; you'll notice how they sound different from the original word!

cub ____________

tap ____________

rip ____________

ban ____________

din ____________

win ____________

tub ____________

MERMAID MATCH

Help Myrtle the Mermaid match the words to the correct pictures. Don't forget to say the words out loud!

book

hoof

cook

glue

room

prunes

broom

blue

RIDDLE ME THIS

Sharky the Shark has some riddles for you. Solve them and read out your answers to him.

I ring in temples, I ring in churches,
I ring in your home and in palaces.
I am a ________.

My sides are round, I'm underground,
And within me, water can be found.
I am a ________.

Supporting buildings, standing tall,
I'm made of bricks; I rhyme with fall.
I am a ________.

Hit me with a bat, or bounce me around,
I'm colourful and oh so round.
I am a ________.

RHYME TIME

Help Ollie the Oyster match the rhyming words.

fish	belly
smile	myrtle
hill	jar
dress	mile
jelly	mess
star	bill
turtle	potter
otter	dish

THE SILENT 'L'

Smiley the Seal wants to use words with a silent 'l'. Can you help him fill in the blanks with the appropriate words?

You ___________ even take a cart.

You ___________ not tell lies.

I ___________ help him myself if I were there.

___________ you look after my fish please?

___________ you please sit down!

We ___________ preserve marine life.

could

would

should

DOBBY'S DILEMMA

Help Dobby the Dolphin fill in the blanks with words from the bubbles. Then, read them out.

I ________ I will learn to swim.

________ was a nice cake.

________ is a nice lake.

What's that roaring noise in the sky? It's ________.

The river ________ flows through London city.

________ Ganges is a sacred river in India.

________ you! I appreciate your kindness.

Trains were not working. ________ we took the bus.

the this that think

thunder therefore thames thank

STARRY SORTER

Starry the Starfish needs to sort his word bubbles. Say the words out loud and match them to the basket whose name rhymes with them.

CONFUSED CHLOE

Chloe the Clownfish is very confused between the letters 'c' and 'k'. Can you help her fill the correct letter in the blank?

______obra	______loud
______oast	______ar

zin______	pin______	______ettle
______olt	broo______	______oo______

TURTLE TALK

Help Toto the Turtle fill in the blanks with words from the shell.

My mother made great __________.

The swordfish seems as if it has a __________ on it.

These animals look like __________.

Never keep animals in __________.

That __________ you see is the light of the fish.

Please be careful on the __________.

That tiny __________ there is a small fish.

That is like a natural __________ in the water.

RHYME TIME

Read the rhyme and circle the rhyming words. Say them out loud.

Under the deep blue sparkling sea
Lives a fish as greedy as can be.

On rotting seaweed he loves to crunch
Apart from the same old fishy munch.

He eats floating tyres and rotting planks too
He once ate a monkey who escaped from the zoo.

He once ate a whole school of clown fish
Because he thought they were a tasty dish.

He ate so much and grew so fat
That he burst into pieces with a big,
loud SPLAT!

WORD BUILDER

Use the letters given on the fish to make your own words in the bubbles. Try to make some rhyming words and connect them to each other.

SORT AHOY!

Connect the words to the correct boat.

cycle

lion

ink

ivory

icy

inch

lady

India

why

baby

cozy

eye

STORY TIME

Complete the story by filling the blanks with words from the jellyfish.

glow allowed window wow now tomorrow fellow eyebrows sailed

We went for a cruise in a ship one night. As we __________, there was a __________ in the dark. We inched our way towards it, with raised __________. The __________ by my side said, "Let's come back __________. "__________ don't panic," I said, "sit by the __________." I __________ myself to be strong. And lo! What a sight! "__________!" a coral in the dark, is what we discovered!

TROUBLESOME TROUT

Terry the Trout jumbled up his words. Can you unscramble the letters to form the correct words? Don't forget to read them out loud!

tbauo	
ttruo	
auotncc	
crdwo	
ourhsd	
dgonru	
lcdou	
daruno	
tnuom	
pdoru	

SPELLING SEA

Help Clara the Crab correct the spellings of the words below.

Word	Correct spelling
eest	
weast	
noth	
sourth	
baloon	
buter	
pleese	
impotant	
surprise	
groop	

WORD LADDER

Help Sharpie the Shark build his word ladder. Change one letter in each word to form a new word.

Cart	Peel	Hurt	Pine	Rose

ANSWERS

Page 2

Page 3

Page 4

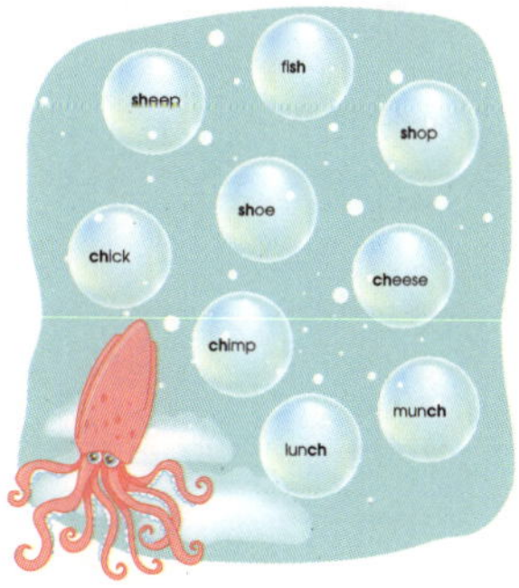

Page 5

Page 6

Page 7

Page 8

Page 9

Page 10

Page 11

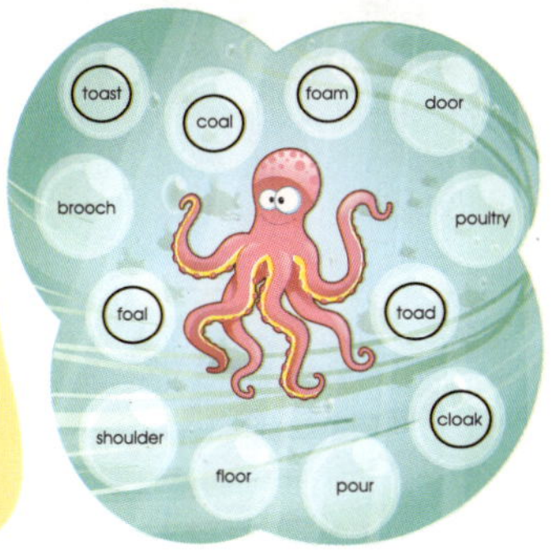

Page 12

Page 13

c	b	t	r	a	i	n	g
l	b	b	c	d	e	f	d
a	l	n	o	w	a	y	e
y	p	m	d	a	y	h	f
q	p	r	s	i	j	i	g
m	a	y	t	t	a	i	l
y	y	z	u	v	w	x	k
a	b	p	l	a	y	c	t
d	e	l	k	l	m	n	r
f	s	a	i	l	p	o	a
p	a	i	l	q	r	s	y
g	h	n	i	s	a	y	j

Page 14

The rabbit's **hair** is furry. (hare/hair)

Here are a **pair** of turtles. (pare/pair)

Help the octopus up these **stairs.** (stairs/stares)

The little jellyfish seems hurt and in **pain.** (pane/pain)

They call her a **plain** fish. (plane/plain)

The lion's **mane** is beautiful. (mane/main).

Page 15

Page 16

Page 17

I ring in temples, I ring in churches,
I ring in your home and in palaces.
I am a **bell.**

My sides are round, I'm underground,
And within me, water can be found.
I am a **well.**

Supporting buildings, standing tall,
I'm made of bricks; I rhyme with fall.
I am a **wall.**

Hit me with a bat, or bounce me around,
I'm colourful and oh so round.
I am a **ball.**

ANSWERS

Page 18

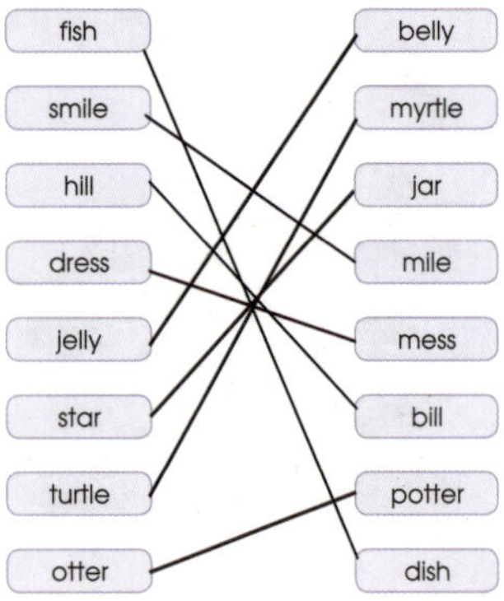

Page 19

You **could** even take a cart.

You **should** not tell lies

I **would** help him myself if I were there.

Could you look after my fish please?

Would you please sit down!

We **should** preserve marine life.

Page 20

I **think** I will learn to swim.

That was a nice cake.

This is a nice lake.

What's that roaring noise in the sky? It's **thunder**.

The river **Thames** flows through London city.

The Ganges is a sacred river in India.

Thank you! I appreciate your kindness.

Trains were not working. **Therefore**, we took the bus.

Page 21

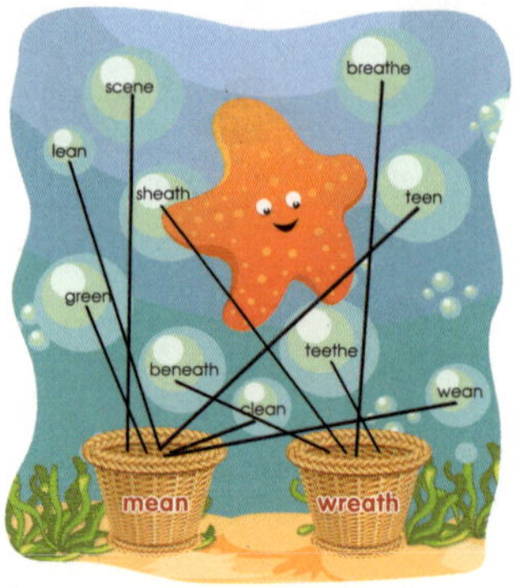

Page 22

cobra

coast

cloud

car

zin**c**

colt

pin**k**

broo**k**

kettle

coo**k**

Page 23

My mother made great **pickle**.

The swordfish seems as if it has a **hammock** on it.

These animals look like **ducks**.

Never keep animals in **shackles**.

That **flicker** you see is the light of the fish.

Please be careful on the **deck**.

That tiny **speck** there is a small fish.

That is like a natural **speck** in the water.

Page 24

Under the deep blue sparkling **sea**
Lives a fish as greedy as can **be**.

On rotting seaweed he loves to **crunch**
Apart from the same old fishy **munch**.

He eats floating tyres and rotting planks **too**
He once ate a monkey who escaped from the **zoo**.

He once ate a whole school of clown **fish**
Because he thought they were a tasty **dish**.

He ate so much and grew so **fat**
That he burst into pieces with a big, loud **SPLAT**!

Page 26

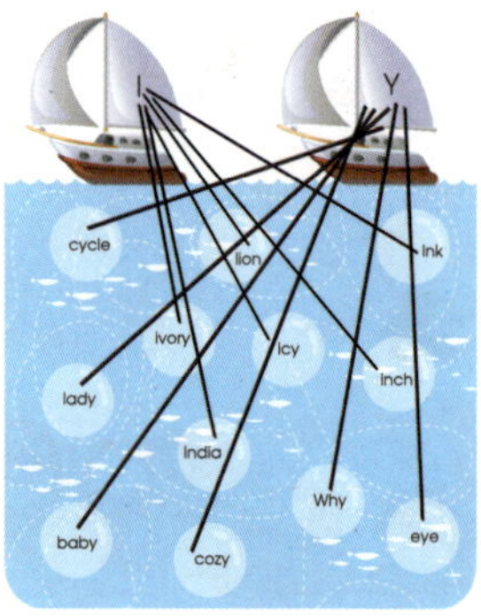

Page 27

glow allowed window

wow now

tomorrow fellow

eyebrows sailed

We went for a cruise in a ship one night. As we **sailed**, there was a **glow** in the dark. We inched our way towards it, with raised **eyebrows**. The **fellow** by my side said, "Let's come back **tomorrow**. "**Now** don't panic," I said, "sit by the **window**." I **allowed** myself to be strong. And lo! What a sight! "**Wow**!" a coral in the dark, is what we discovered!

Page 28

t b a u o	**about**
t t r u o	**trout**
a u o t n c c	**account**
c r d w o	**crowd**
o u r h s d	**shroud**
d g o n r u	**ground**
l c d o u	**cloud**
d a r u n o	**around**
t n u o m	**mount**
p d o r u	**proud**

Page 29

eest	**east**
weast	**west**
noth	**north**
sourth	**south**
baloon	**balloon**
buter	**butter**
pleese	**please**
Impotant	**important**
surpise	**surprise**
groop	**group**